FORCE-ON-FORCE GUNFIGHT TRAINING

FORCE-ON-FORCE GUNFIGHT TRAINING

The Interactive, Reality-Based Solution

Gabriel Suarez

Paladin Press • Boulder, Colorado

Also by Gabriel Suarez:

Close-Range Gunfighting (video)
Combative Perspective
The Tactical Advantage
The Tactical Advantage: The Video
The Tactical Pistol (also available in Spanish)
Tactical Pistol Marksmanship
Tactical Rifle
The Tactical Shotgun

Force-on-Force Gunfight Training:
The Interactive, Reality-Based Solution
by Gabriel Suarez

Copyright © 2005 by Gabriel Suarez

ISBN 13: 978-1-58160-474-0
Printed in the United States of America

Published by Paladin Press, a division of
Paladin Enterprises, Inc.
Gunbarrel Tech Center
7077 Winchester Circle
Boulder, Colorado 80301 USA
+1.303.443.7250

Direct inquiries and/or orders to the above address.

Visit our Web site at www.paladin-press.com

TABLE OF CONTENTS

PREFACE

The terms *reality*, *real world*, and *reality-based* have become modern labels that designate a departure from the theoretical or the artificial, a move toward a more pragmatic view of things. When the subject is combat training, reality-based means that the course and the instructor are focused on making the students better fighters in the environments and situations where fights are actually likely to occur, and not on teaching theoretical or sporting-based applications.

In the past, whether in the combatives/martial arts world or in the defensive shooting community, there was great deal of theorizing. I believe this was mainly because few trainers had any actual combat experience. (Most sane people, after all, spend their lives trying to avoid trouble rather than looking for it.) Their focus tended to be on their particular area of expertise and on things other than actual combat skill development. For example, a given martial arts school might have had a competitive focus, a spiritual/meditative focus, or even a cultural/traditional focus, rather than a focus on destroying one's attackers.

In the shooting community, similar agendas prevailed. Despite the prevalence of shooting schools that promoted themselves as "reality-based," there was still a focus on simply passing a certain course of fire or dealing with a particular shooting drill. Such schools were actually focused on sports, for example, or on something other than combat success. Typically, students viewed what they shot at as a "target," and not as a representation of an enemy.

Please understand that I have nothing against these hobbies or pastimes. Often they serve as the place where foundational skills are learned, without which further learning cannot occur. Nonetheless, if the objective is combat ability, the martial gymnast or the tactical bull's-eye shooter will

Reality training comes to the art of the gun—Interactive Gunfighting training.

inevitably find himself lacking at the moment of truth. As Bruce Lee once said, "Bags don't hit back." Likewise, as applied to the shooter, paper targets don't shoot back.

In the martial arts world, the "reality revolution" started when the Gracie family choked out traditional fighter after traditional fighter in the Ultimate Fighting Championships (UFC), at the time the most unrestricted fight sport in the civilized world. The defeated paragons of the "partial arts" soon learned that their mysterious "death touch" techniques didn't work as well on noncompliant men beating their faces in with elbow smashes or choking them to within seconds of unconsciousness as they did on the indoctrinated students in their home dojos. The coup d'état had begun.

Today, the sources and variety of reality-based martial training have skyrocketed. No more are combat-skill-seeking students required to wax floors or paint fences in voluntary servitude in the hopes of getting a crumb of combat knowledge that falls off the table of some *untested* combat master. Today, you pay for a lesson in reality fighting and learn real, kickass stuff that will work for you that evening should you become the target of thugs. No temple mumbo jumbo, just pure, useful combat skills.

In the shooting community, the change has been more gradual. Many shooting schools and instructors are still indirectly (some unconsciously) competition-oriented. In truth, many of the doctrines that motivated and influenced tactical shooting as we know it today came from the competitive community. The following are two notable examples:

1) Police Practical Pistol Competition (PPC) influenced police officer gunfight training for decades. PPC is basically bull's-eye shooting with a service revolver and has very little to do with actual gunfighting.

2) The Bear Valley Gunslingers and the competitive activities of the early 1960s directly influenced Jeff

Cooper's Modern Technique of the Pistol. Cooper's conclusions from those days in turn heavily influenced International Practical Shooting Competition (IPSC). IPSC in turn, eventually, influenced police and military training.

There is nothing wrong with competition, since those seeking competitive acclaim usually develop a very high level of marksmanship skill. But that alone is not sufficient. Gunfighting and killing have only certain things coincidentally in common with competitive shooting. A kickboxing champion may be a good man to have beside you in a bar fight, but perhaps not. Similarly, an IPSC champion may be a good man to have with you in a close-range gunfight, but maybe not. I know several high-level competitive shooters who do not even carry a pistol. It's a matter of mental focus and purpose . . . among other things.

Many competitive shooters are gun focused and shoot at paper targets rather than at representations and pictures of their adversaries. The focus is not necessarily on winning a fight but on quick marksmanship, which is a part, but not the whole. Some competitions do not even permit humanoid targets! Even the most powerful political organization for shooters, the NRA, though it publishes the monthly "Armed Citizen" column in its magazines, is often loath to acknowledge that guns are weapons and are used by good guys and girls to shoot and kill evil men every day.

Moreover, although many trainers have extensive marksmanship skills, few have any actual combat experience; nor are they exposed to the studies of those who do have such experience. And while marksmanship is important, knowing how to fight an adversary, as any properly trained martial artist would, is an essential aspect of gunfight training. Unfortunately, few gun trainers have any interest in moving beyond the level at which their own training and skill are stuck. It's an ego thing for many, and they seek to convince their students that nothing beyond what they can offer is needed.

One example that was related to me involved a world-famous trainer being asked about weapon-retention techniques in close quarters. The "guru" gave an impatient look and replied, "Why don't you just shoot him?" The comment was followed by snickers of amusement from the guru's devoted fans in the class. The very valid question was left unanswered because the guru does not know the first thing about retaining his weapon in a fight. The real loss, of course, is that another student is out on the street without the right tools to win a fight.

There are other trainers who trust only those in uniform and refuse to teach anything beyond basic target shooting to the lowly and untrustworthy civilian. They seem to forget that this is America and that Americans (especially today) have a clear and present need to learn these skills.

Another issue is that many of the safety constraints necessary when training on a shooting range with live-fire guns preclude the flexibility and freedom of movement that are necessary in an actual fight. Yet the range is the only area where most trainers operate, and thus the full development of the art of the gun has been held back by a reluctance to leave that comfortable environment.

Contrary to the advice sometimes given by well-meaning but uninformed trainers, sometimes you can't "just shoot them," and you must rely on other means to win the confrontation.

I was once called a "pot-stirrer looking for a better

Square-range training is essential to the full development of a shooter, but the development must not stop there.

way." I think that describes the focus here. I hope my studies make the "powerful movers" of the training community really uncomfortable. I hope they stay up at night worrying about where the reality-based trainers are moving the art. I hope their students go and train with the progressive trainers and leave the dinosaur perspective behind. In doing so they will become more complete fighters, move the art forward, and have a greater chance of success when the Final Exam comes to them.

Is square range (shooting range) training worthless? *Absolutely not.* But neither is it the zenith of the art. Although a man or woman can go to a marksmanship school, never take another step beyond that, and have that skill level serve

This Interactive Gunfighting student shows perfect form as he gets off the line of attack and, seeing "meat and metal" superimposed on his stationary adversary's chest, fires at him.

him or her satisfactorily in a defensive encounter, the objective of writing this book and conducting this type of training is to develop the art beyond the level of "average adequacy" so often embraced by those who seek to dumb things down for the uninterested lowest-common-denominator shooter. The objective is to advance the art.

The complete gunfighter learns the mechanics of his weapon. He learns to manage it and operate it with grace, fluidity, and reflexive action. And he learns to fire it with requisite accuracy for the problem at hand. He learns all these things on the firing range with relatively traditional (and not so traditional) methods. But once he has acquired these skills, there must be an evolution beyond the firing

Square-range training is what prepares you in part for interactive training. These shooters learn how to respond from and fight in confined spaces, such as in an automobile.

range. The firing range will then become a source of technical skill maintenance.

The gunfighter trainee must begin training with replica firearms against live human adversaries in situations replicating those he is likely to face in a real confrontation. First, this is done in very controlled and designed drills similar to those seen in reality-based martial arts schools. This accustoms the trainee to what a human being (as opposed to an IPSC target) looks like in his gun sights. It gets him used to moving and maneuvering around an adversary and lends a sense of reality to what has previously been a technical exercise. Next these techniques are applied in carefully implemented scenarios.

In this book, I will show why range training is only a first step and why force-on-force (interactive) training is essential to the complete development of the gunfighter. I will also elaborate on how to develop and implement such training, including safety issues and equipment concerns.

Force-on-force interactive training and integrated force training are the future of the reality-based art of the gun. The pot has been stirred and a better way found. There can be no going back. I hope you enjoy the ride.

DYNAMICS OF A REAL GUNFIGHT VS. RANGE DRILLS

The reality and violence of a real street fight cannot be duplicated on the firing range with any target system or any drill.

Today, there is a great deal of data on the dynamics of an armed confrontation. Some of it comes from the firsthand accounts of those who have been there and done that. Their stories, whether from Costa Rica, Colombia, or Los Angeles, are all dramatically similar.

The FBI's Uniform Crime Report (UCR) offers a wealth of information, and its points about the dynamics of armed confrontations have changed very little in the time it has been available. In a nutshell, armed confrontations happen suddenly, at close range, often in reduced light, and are likely to involve multiple adversaries. The one problem with the UCR is that it focuses exclusively on law enforcement personnel. Suarez International, USA is not a police training organization. Sure, we train soldiers and cops, but we also train private citizens in the same exact stuff. Although the "dynamics of encounter" for civilians are similar to those for law enforcement in some respects, they are different in the sense that police officers often know they are going into a dangerous environment, whereas private citizens would avoid such situations. Thus, the element of surprise working against the private citizen is often greater than that working against the officer.

Moreover, the statistics compiled by the FBI are based on officers that were killed. Thus, as harsh as it may sound, potentially they are the statistics of failure. At this time, I am not aware of any agency or study group maintaining statistics on fights that were won. A comparison of such data with the FBI's UCR would be an invaluable resource. Alas, the nature of American police administrations is that they focus on failures and ignore successes. Fortuitous outcomes reinforce poor tactics and training.

Another viable source of information is the timeless "Armed Citizen" column published in the NRA magazines *America's First Freedom* and *American Rifleman* on a monthly basis. It describes situations in which citizens successfully defended themselves and their homes with a firearm. Notice I said "defended themselves," not just "fired at their attackers." In the real world, many more attacks are prevented by the ready presence of a gun than are solved with gunfire.

Finally, your daily newspaper and the nightly news can provide you with valuable trends in the patterns of attacks. Today the enemy might just as easily be a jihadist looking for the magic carpet ride to paradise as a meth addict looking for a few bucks, a child molester looking to kidnap a child, or an urban gang member looking to expand his turf.

The dynamics of each of these hypothetical situations are very similar. In most cases a private citizen will not be going out looking for a gunfight. The only instance that I can think of where this is a likely choice is the *preemptive ambush,* or a *family hostage-rescue,* where a citizen is protecting against home invaders and, in essence, taking the fight to them before they can overpower the household. In most other cases, a private individual will seek avoidance and disengagement as the first option. An alert mental attitude and the ability to disengage and evade have ended many more fights (before they've begun) than any fast and accurate shot.

Thus, the armed private citizen, if he fights, will find himself in the fight with little or no warning. He may have been targeted for a number of reasons:

1) He looked like an easy mark and had something the bad guys wanted. Solution: don't look like an easy mark.

2) He was targeted by the terrorist/kidnapper/robber for sociopolitical reasons. In some parts of the country, a well-dressed businessman venturing out after dark might as well have a bull's-eye painted on his chest. (Hey, that's reality, folks. If it offends you, perhaps you are being too naive about modern life.) Double that risk for a woman. The solution is obviously to remain aware about where you are and what is going on around you. Additionally, do not rationalize away things that concern you or seem out of place. In *The Combative Perspective*, I discussed *situational awareness* at length. The topic applies here. Don't assume anything. Most of all, remember where you are and who you are. Realize who is around you. The combination of these three factors can often add up to a very hazardous situation. Am I suggesting that you profile those around you? *Absolutely!* We all have a very good sense of what the bad guys look like, how they act, and how they dress. Profile the hell out of everyone. Anyone who does not profile today is stupid.

3) He stumbled into an in-progress crime. How many people have walked right into a robbery in progress or

another type of crime? Hundred of thousands of folks all over the world get into trouble every year for just that reason.

Each of the above-mentioned situations can potentially be avoided by being alert, noticing the telltale clues that signal some impending trouble, and, when possible, disengaging. But disengaging isn't always possible. We'll talk about that too.

The dynamics of a confrontation that starts out as I have just described have remained virtually unchanged for decades. Why? Because men have not changed the way they fight against each other. They are as follows:

The fight will likely be very close. Here an Interactive Gunfighting student defends against a knife attacker. Not exactly the sort of thing you can do on a shooting range.

This photo shows the relationship between good guy and bad guy at the traditional range distance of seven yards. It sure seems like a long way, doesn't it? Most confrontations happen at a much closer range.

1) **The fight will be close-range.** I don't mean seven yards (the distance where most shooting schools prepare you to fight), but more like seven feet. Often it will begin at arm's range, beginning as a fistfight, or a "mad dogging" session.

2) **There will often be at least two adversaries, sometimes more.** The bad guys know there is strength in numbers.

5

More often than not, you will be facing multiple adversaries. Do you know how to really survive such an event?

3) **Low-light confrontations are very likely**. Because we venture out after dark so often in urban areas, and the bad guy seeks the cover darkness provides, the lighting conditions are likely to be poor. How dark is your house at 3 A.M.?

4) **There is a good chance that you may be totally unprepared—that is, not expecting a fight.** If you have a pistol with you, it will probably be carried concealed; thus the one-second draw you routinely do on the shooting range may be a bit slower.

Although some of these *dynamics* can be prepared for on a shooting range or simulated in a shoot house, the incident

6

You may not even be ready for it. Do you have the skills to fight at all engagement ranges?

itself can only be duplicated safely by using training guns such as Airsoft. To achieve the latter, many of the artificial "range safety" rules that are observed when training on a shooting range *must be set aside*.

The basics, such as keeping the finger off the trigger until you've made a conscious decision to shoot, being certain of your adversary before firing, and so on, are easily maintained in combat. Other rules specifically designed to run a safe firing line may seem essential on the range but are ludicrous in a gunfight. They are essential on the shooting range because a mistake with a live loaded weapon can have tragic results. On the other hand, in a fight, winning it takes precedence over notions like not covering suspected adversaries with a gun muzzle, not breaking the 180-degree line, and so on.

Square-range marksmanship training is important to developing necessary skills, learning how to hit with speed and accuracy, and learning how to run your gun. But training exclusively on the shooting range for the development of marksmanship is not sufficient to prepare you for in-your-face, arm's-length combat against a live human being bent on your destruction.

Some trainers and schools realize the deficiencies of exclusive square-range marksmanship training and seek to devise ingenious target systems and exhaustive technical drills in the hopes of replicating what the real world will bring. Unfortunately, they fall short of replicating what your actual enemy will do and act like.

I have seen dummies dressed up in clothing with plastic guns taped to their hands and mounted on springs in an effort

The only way to truly prepare for a street fight is through a complete training program that covers all the angles. A training program must contain an element of force-on-force.

8

to simulate movement. Unfortunately, no inanimate piece of plastic or paper will ever truly replicate a human adversary. No matter how you dress it up, how you position it in a shoot house, what you tape to its hands, or how you make it bob and weave, nothing can truly duplicate a human enemy. Your real "target" is not an inanimate piece of plastic or cardboard but rather another man like you who for some reason has selected you as *his* target. It's about fighting, not just shooting.

Another area where mistakes are made in training is in the design of movers, or moving targets. There are elaborate machines designed to run a target toward you at high speed. Students are told to try to outdraw the rapidly advancing target, but they are not permitted to move. *Why not?* Well, because it would cause shots to go into the mover's machinery or otherwise be outside the intended impact area. Range gizmos like these reinforce incorrect tactics (such as holding your ground under attack instead off moving off line) that could potentially get you killed. Avoid them!

So how do we train realistically enough to be able to fight well in the real world? The answer lies in leaving the square range, leaving the live-fire training method, leaving the actual firearm, and moving into the world of interactive training, aka force-on-force (FOF).

2

THE FORCE-
ON-FORCE
SOLUTION

The more realistic your training is, the
more comfortable you will be operating in dangerous environments.

There are three parts to a successful gunfighting training
program: dry-practice training drills, actual live fire on the
shooting range, and FOF.

Think of dry practice in the same sense as you would a
shadowboxing drill. In this type of training, the boxer con-
nects different combinations of movements in order to develop a feel for, and muscle memory of, the basics of his fighting
system. Dry practice does the same thing for a shooter.

Live fire on a paper or steel target is akin to a heavy-bag
workout in boxing. During heavy-bag training a fighter develops real power and gets a feel for what actually hitting something is like. The shooter learns to control recoil and work out
minor issues with regard to grip, position, sighting issues, and
so on. A great deal of development can take place at this junc-

11

ture. A fighter who does nothing but work on shadowboxing and bag drills can certainly defend himself well enough in a fight. Similarly, a gunman who has dedicated himself to extensive dry-practice and shooting drills can do reasonably well in a fight. But this point in the training certainly does not represent the zenith of a warrior's development.

The boxer will eventually need to spar with someone, and the gunfighter must learn what another living man looks like at gunpoint (even if only within the training environment).

Experience is an essential part of the warrior's development. Yet real combat experience is something most normal people would prefer to avoid. I spent my years in uniform seeking out and accruing experience in this area. I do not rec-

Interactive Gunfighting students learn how to hit quickly and on the move while avoiding being hit themselves. This gives them a combative perspective that the targets on the firing range can never provide.

ommend it to others, but I would not trade these experiences for anything. They gave me a perspective, almost at the cost of my own life, that I could not have received anywhere else. The price is high, and the risks are great. Ideally, you want to accrue such experience without much risk.

The boxer gains this kind of experiential knowledge through sparring. He knows that he will not get killed in the ring, but the real exchange of blows gives him a combative perspective that the bag can never provide. The shooter can accrue this kind of empirical knowledge through FOF training.

Facing a tactical drill where you have a live adversary to deal with, or shoot at, creates a greater feeling of stress than the most difficult of square-range drills. It's a training session, so you know death is not going to be the price for a mistake, but you also know that missed shots, or poorly executed tactics, will result in your being shot by the adversary—a slightly painful experience even with an Airsoft gun.

Thus the trainee gunfighter reaps the benefits of experience and practical knowledge without the constraints of the range—and without having to risk his life. FOF training will revolutionize your skills as well as your entire perspective on defending yourself with a pistol.

3

THE ROLE OF THE ANTAGONIST (BAD GUY)

Say hello to the bad guy—a bad-guy role player awaits his cue to attack.

One of the controversies and source of potential problems in FOF training is the antagonist role-player, or "bad guy." FOF systems such as Airsoft, or even the marking cartridges popular with police agencies, do not provide one vital element of true gunfights, and that is *the ballistic effect*.

A role-player who wishes to can receive a frightening number of hits from any of these systems and still keep fighting, even though in real life he would most likely have succumbed to his wounds.

In a real event, a man who gets shot several times in the face will have some sort of adverse reaction and in most cases will stop aggressive action. We've all heard the horror stories of the bad guy who absorbed a platoon's worth of lead and still kept driving on, but that is not going to happen each and every

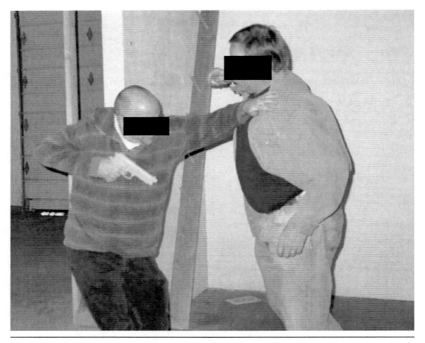

The student playing the part of the antagonist must understand what his role is in the overall training plan.

time you shoot a man. If it were the norm, we would leave our Glocks at home and go back to carrying swords and axes.

Thus, in FOF, despite the fact that he is physically capable of continuing the fight, the bad guy must "die." The scenario must have a plausible and obtainable conclusion to it.

The objective is to learn in as realistic (in terms of stress and dynamics) an environment as can be safely provided without the real risk of actual injury or death. Should it get the heart pumping and the nerves frayed? Sure. But picture this extreme: a good-guy role-player and a bad-guy role-player face off and go to guns. Each is getting good hits on the other, and neither will give ground because they do not want to *program a quitting attitude*. After several seconds, both are

The bad guy/aggressor must give the trainee a good presentation of what a street attacker would do.

standing facing each other with empty guns and welts all over their bodies. What was the point of the lesson or exercise? What did they learn?

Errr, ahhh, hmmmm . . . oh yes—gunfights are dangerous! OK, so what? We knew that from the beginning. The only thing these guys learned was to shoot fast while getting hit. Until some mad scientist develops FOF technology that will in effect "knock you out" when it hits you, there is only so much we can do. So since current FOF technology lacks the true ballistic effect, we must simulate it by having one party react as if he's been shot.

Now there are some points that must be remembered here. The good guy in the scenario must always keep fighting no matter what. He must never be conditioned to stop or quit. Even if he's been hit so many times that he looks like he robbed a nest of killer bees, he must keep fighting. As my spec-ops friends say, "FIDO" (F—- It, Drive On). If he makes mistakes, they will be discussed in the debriefing.

What about the bad guy? Let me point out that the purpose of FOF training is threefold. One is to expose untested personnel to the stress and dynamics of a real gunfight. Two is to break out of the square-range box by working in an environment more like the real world. Three is to learn to use correct techniques learned on the range in that environment.

The scenarios are not designed to be no-win situations; nor are they designed to make everyone fail (what good is any training if this is the case?). And neither is the scenario intended specifically to train the bad guy, or to show who is the baddest dude in the class. Thus, unless the good guy does something really stupid, he should be able to win the scenario, at least initially. There are different levels to these scenarios.

So basically, the bad guy must put his ego and his desire to win aside and stick to the script, thereby helping his training partner learn. Thus, a bad-guy role-player is not a cotrainee in the fight, but rather just a "sparring partner."

Actually, "sparring partner" is a good analogy. Think of the world champion kickboxer in training. Much of his training involves sparring in the ring with various partners. The job of these sparring partners is to help prepare the champ for his next match, not to try to kick his ass every time they step into the ring with him. Sparring partners with such an ego-based, headhunting agenda will quickly be asked to leave by the champ's manager. Get the picture? Without a good bad guy, the scenario will not teach anything to anyone and will leave everyone frustrated and confused.

So where can we find such good bad guys?

One solution is to hire them. Many large, fixed-location schools specializing in "adrenal stress training" (actual hands-on fistfighting combat with armored opponents) have a group of trained, professional, paid, and very able role-playing bad guys. The drawback to this in the gunfighting arena is cost. Because the training must often be done at a specific location, and since a great deal of equipment is involved, the travel arrangements for the entire FOF trainer's entourage would become prohibitively expensive. As an example, a three-day class involving two dedicated role-players and one instructor would cost upwards of $1,200 per student to make it economically feasible! Undoubtedly some students would pay that, but not many.

Another option is to use students themselves as role-players. The first advantage to this is that a two- or three-day training session will cost the students a fraction of what the other class would cost. Second, if the student role-player will set his ego and desire to win aside, the scenario will be as much a learning experience for him as for his good-guy opponent. Last, it teaches all of the students how to organize their own continuing training.

The bad-guy role-player must have a realistic goal. That is, he must act and "think" as a bad guy would. Why would a criminal break in to your house? Would it be to hide in a room and lie in wait for you for hours? And would your mission always be to "go on the hunt for him"? Possibly, but I suspect stuff like that only happens at shooting schools with a limited base of knowledge in their instructional staff.

A bad guy has a mission. He is breaking in to your home to do something—probably steal, rape, or kill. He is entering your business armed and with friends to intimidate you into compliance under the threat of death. What is the true bad guy's mission? A good bad-guy role-player determines this, accepts the mission, and then follows what it dictates.

As the good guy, your mission will very rarely (only in extreme situations) call for going and searching for him. In your home your mission may be to secure your family and then lie in wait for him. In your business it may be to feign compliance and suddenly ambush or counterattack. So in

FOF training, the good-guy role-player must use his head, keep it real, and avoid letting it become a game.

The key points for students to remember when role-playing in a group class are as follows:

Good guys—use your tactics, keep it real in terms of your mission, and even if you make a mistake, keep fighting; never quit. Errors will be discussed afterward.

Bad guys—you'll get your chance to be the good guy! When you are temporarily given the role of bad guy, put your ego aside and stick to the script. In a group class, it's about everyone, not just about you. If you want it to be just about you, set up a private lesson. Stay with the script!

4

THE MISSION OF THE GOOD GUY

Be aggressive, be dangerous, make the bad guys be afraid of you, and most of all, never, never, never quit!

The bad guy is supposed to act like a bad guy. He has a bad guy's mission to fulfill when confronted by the good guy, and he is to exhibit a scripted reaction when shot, challenged, or ignored. In a perfect scenario handled adroitly by the good guy student, the bad guy should lose. If the bad guy fails to exhibit an effect when shot, the scenario loses realism and takes on a gamelike air. A friend who once worked for Uncle Sugar in an OPFOR (Opposing Force) capacity in the training of American troops told me that if he and his guys did their job they portrayed enemy forces correctly and lost the battle more often than not. Much the same can be said for civilian FOF. The bad-guy role-player's mission is to portray a bad guy and lose the fight.

The good guy has a mission as well.

21

The good guy must use the techniques he has studied in live-fire training on the square range. If those techniques do not work, they should be discarded and replaced with workable ones. The good guy never quits; no matter if he's made an error and has been peppered with pellets, he keeps fighting.

First of all, we need to develop in him the attitude that as long as he is breathing, he will keep fighting. The good guy *never gives up!* Instructors who teach students to give up mid-scenario when a mistake is observed are doing their charges a grave disservice.

One gunfight survivor was once asked how he could possibly keep shooting after he himself had been shot. "That's easy," he replied, "I wasn't out of ammo, and I hadn't been killed yet." Even if he is shot, the good guy keeps fighting. If his gun doesn't work and cannot be fixed immediately, the good guy goes for a second gun or a training blade. In high-level simulations, he may smash his fist into the bad-guy role-player's protective face mask. The good guy never, never, never, never quits. Get it?!

Second, the good guy needs to have clarity of mission. What is he trying to do? A man searching a house for a suspect will use different tactics than a man fighting to get to his kid's room to rescue him. The majority of students who attend my courses are private citizens, corporate protection specialists, or individual operators. (Occasionally we train SWAT teams, but the focus is on the individual.) I teach them the skills they need, and then the scenarios they face as individuals are organized to be realistic for their operational needs.

To send a man into an FOF scenario with the instructions "go find the bad guy" is overly simplistic, unrealistic, and indicative of a lazy trainer. *Why am I going in there again?* When the student answers that, the tactics will be obvious. An individual good guy may be

- Searching his home or business for an intruder
- Moving to rescue family during a beak-in home invasion

The event is debriefed immediately afterward while the lessons are still fresh in everyone's minds.

- Moving to rescue coworkers during an active shooter event
- Resisting a holdup/takeover terrorist event
- Resisting a kidnapping/terrorist hostage-taking attempt
- Moving to secure family in a safe room

The actions in each of these examples will be vastly different in terms of speed, aggressiveness, and tactics. Nonetheless, there is a clear and specific objective or mission for the good guy. For example, if his objective is to move from the master bedroom to his child's room and hold his ground there, and he is able to do so without shooting the bad guy, he has still accomplished his mission. *Thus his mission may or may not call for shooting the bad guy.*

Finally, the good guy *must learn* from the scenario. Training this way is certainly fun, but the object is also to test students' tactics and what they've trained on the square range in a pseudo-uncontrolled environment. Thus, how it works in simulated gunfights is indicative of its viability in actual gunfights. The training may highlight mistake after mistake, or it may show the trainee is training correctly, but it must show something.

5

MARKING OR NONMARKING?

The Airsoft pistols are ultra-realistic in size, weight, and dimensions.

All areas of study create controversy. In FOF, the controversy is marking cartridges vs. nonmarking cartridges. The proponents of the former dismiss Airsoft because the pellets do not mark you with a paint spot in the way something like a Simunitions marking round would. In the opposite camp are those, myself included, who question the importance of a mark resulting from a shot that hits.

In an environment where participants' competitive spirit surpasses their desire to learn, it may be necessary to have a red mark that satisfies the childish "I got you, no you didn't" mentality. This is especially so in some "professional" schools where there is no pain penalty because the participants in the scenario/drill are so armored and padded up that they wouldn't even feel a real bullet. They can't feel the impact when an adversary hits them.

Some companies that manufacture marking cartridges for

this training require so-called safety procedures so onerous that they simply cannot be maintained without sacrificing the momentum and quality of the class. These include limits on contact distances that preclude simulating a realistic confrontation (in terms of typical distances of conflict). The only advantage marking cartridges offer is the ability to visibly demonstrate the impacts with residual paint at the point of contact.

With Airsoft there is no mark, but its advantages surpass the training benefits of other simulation systems. The benefits of Airsoft are as follows:

- Airsoft guns are intended to be high-priced toys. They are not real firearms modified for the marking rounds but rather manufactured replicas intended to be used with plastic pellets.
- Airsoft, unlike firearms modified for marking cartridges, are unregulated and thus can be owned by anyone and trained with in the most oppressive, liberty-averse, backward areas of the nation. Compare this to companies that only sell their marking cartridges and conversion kits to police agencies.
- Airsoft is a clean training tool. The pellets will not mark up a building with red paint on the wall or litter the floor with brass cases. After a training session, a shop vacuum cleaner easily picks up all the evidence. This makes it possible to train in venues that are true to real life, as opposed to being restricted to a range.
- Airsoft can be fired at training partners at point-blank distances without injury, enabling safe training to take place at correct intervals of distance.
- The minimal safety gear (face mask, long-sleeved sweatshirt, and gloves) required with Airsoft allows for immediate indication of mistakes while remaining economical. An Airsoft gun along with the safety gear mentioned above costs less than half the price of a new pistol. Thus all can benefit from FOF training.

- Trainers using products prohibited for civilian training are paying top dollar for the marking cartridges and the conversion kits in backdoor, black-market purchases. Airsoft guns provide the same training effects for everyone at less than half the cost.
- Marking cartridges have a shelf life that limits their stockpile storage. No such limits exist for Airsoft.

Clearly, the advantages of using Airsoft are many. The only perceived disadvantage is the inability to mark the bad guy when a shot is delivered, yet this is only an issue when a trainee's ego is such that he must have his mistakes shown to him in an undeniable manner (i.e., with the presence of a red paint mark on his armor). A dynamic trainer who is comfortable with his own gunfighting ability should be able to point out the folly of such an approach to someone like this. If said student still wants to argue, the same trainer can politely point him toward the door.

The objective of a training event is to teach the students how to prevail in the dangerous situations they are training for. A trainee going into an Airsoft scenario with a long-sleeved shirt will know perfectly well when, where, and how he is hit with a pellet—there is no need for paint marks. He will have instant feedback because he will literally *feel* his mistakes, whereas the trainee using the liability-averse company's marking cartridges will not—that is, unless he risks violating the company's safety policies by leaving his armor off (not a wise idea in litigious America).

When you factor in the added advantages of using no live-fire weapons (converted or not), utilizing close-range drills, and equipping a small group with Airsoft training gear for the price of one marking cartridge conversion kit, the choice is clear. Airsoft is safer, more efficient, more economical, and available to everyone. In my opinion, it is the future of true gunfight tactical training, especially for the armed private citizen.

6

THE LEVELS OF SIMULATION— HOW HARD DO YOU WANT TO GO?

How hard do you want to go? Here an Interactive Gunfight student is really trying to hit the other student with a rubber training knife. Had the student in black not been able to successfully implement a defense, he would have had his training mask knocked right off his face.

There are different levels of training in the use of the firearm for self-defense. A beginning shooter learns how to operate his pistol safely. He learns marksmanship first, and then, as progress is made, greater development occurs. He learns to draw and shoot fast and accurately. He learns to move tactically with the pistol and, as the competitors say, to race the gun. As skill improves, he gets to go into a shoot house and accomplish more tactical things. Notice that there is a building-block approach to things here. The same progression must occur with FOF training.

A few years ago there was a training company that specialized in placing marksmen in scenarios using paintball guns and then simply shooting them into a mass of paint goo submission on the first go-around. Their thinking was that such

These Interactive Gunfight students move through a close-range confrontation evolution known as static line drills, which will make them more comfortable with the real-world application of their range skills.

is how a gunfight is and that the students needed to understand that. In my opinion, this was a mistake, since the students learned nothing other than the fact that gunfights are dangerous. The equivalent of this on the shooting range would be to ask a man who has just been given his first pistol to shoot a sub-six-second El Presidente! At best, it would be a discouraging exercise in futility.

In that sense, FOF training is the same. The trainee must build up to the level where he can benefit from the training event. For any development to occur, there must be an understanding of the levels of simulation. Skill development and preparation for the gunfight are the goals. There must be a link between the shooting range and what the trainee will be expected to do in FOF. Thus a progression of skill-building drills must be followed in order for trainees to gain maximum benefit from FOF training.

LEVEL ONE: STATIC LINE DRILLS

The transition from square range to FOF is a critical point in training. Some trainers like to take students who may be very good shots or graduates from marksmanship-oriented schools and thrust them unprepared into a force-on-force environment. Predictably, such students fail miserably because they have never had to shoot anything other than a piece of paper.

When asked the purpose of such a guaranteed-to-fail drill, the instructor usually answers that it will show the trainee how dangerous real fights are. No s*#t, Sherlock! Didn't we already know that? As with training for anything, whether it's gunfighting or auto racing, it's essential to build a foundation of skills before pushing the limits.

In level one the trainee is exposed to drilling with a live human training partner. This is akin to the one-step drills or technique drills in a martial combat school. The trainee now gets to do everything he learned in live-fire on the square range against another man with an Airsoft training gun.

We begin at seven yards. One man is armed with a rubber

During the line drills, we visit the famous Teuller drill, except that this time it's a man and not a target you face.

The Teuller drill is commonly examined at 21 feet. This is a very optimistic distance when discussing urban gunfights. We close the gap incrementally until the knife man is literally right on top of the trainee, and he must then rely on combatives skills to open the door to his gun.

training knife, the other with an Airsoft pistol set up to function with gas only (no pellets). On *go*, the knife man charges the gun man with the intent of slapping the rubber blade right across the gun man's face. If the gun man doesn't move, his safety mask will get knocked right off by the rubber knife. The gun man's goal is to move off line as he draws, evading the knife man and getting his gun out and shooting.

Students of the gunfighting art will recognize this as the famous Teuller drill. But we don't stop there. We decrease the distance incrementally from seven yards to more realistic confrontation distances. Eventually, the trainees realize that there is a point at which they cannot outdraw the knife man,

If you don't move off line, you will be shot. Period.

Move!

and they must begin integrating combatives in addition to moving to avoid getting "cut."

I've seen multiple distinguished graduates of the famous marksmanship-oriented schools get slapped with the knife repeatedly when stubbornness and ego win out over common sense ("Gosh darn it, I'll make this draw fast enough or die trying!") When we take the gun out of their hands and ask them to react as if they were unarmed, suddenly they want to move off line really bad. A ha! We give them their gun back and say, "Do the same thing, but this time shoot him." Lightbulbs go off in previously closed, doctrinal minds. Movement is good!

The drills are repeated against multiple adversaries, since facing more than one adversary in a gunfight is statistically likely.

We repeat the exercise with both men armed with gas-only Airsoft pistols. One man plays the part of the bad guy and gets to move first, but he must remain stationary after that, allowing the trainee (good guy) to learn the benefits of moving on the draw. The good guy keys off his adversary's hand reaching for the gun to move off line and respond. Just as before, we decrease the distance incrementally.

Both exercises are then repeated with two against one or three against one. They are short-duration but very intense versions of the same exercises students practice on the firing range. They serve to familiarize the trainee with the dynamics of combat versus the requirements of marksmanship.

Both exercises also bring the trainee uncomfortably clos-

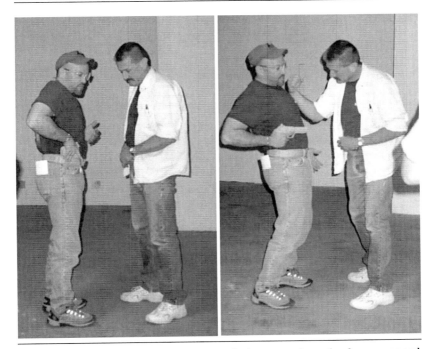

Traditionally popular close-quarters techniques, such as the famous speed rock, prove worthless when we leave paper targets and begin to work with live adversaries in gunfight simulations.

er to his adversary/training partner. Many trainers advocate the "distance is your friend" mentality. That mantra is no solace to the man who must fight in an elevator, toilet stall, or phone booth, or to the protective agent who can't create distance in a crowd lest he leave his charge behind. Distance is something to be controlled, nothing more and nothing less.

To train at face-to-face intervals, we deactivate the slide stop feature on the Airsoft guns with a small piece of duct tape or electrical tape. (Some of our school guns have had the slide stop device internally deactivated.) This allows us to load the Airsoft magazine with gas, but no pellets. This will allow the pistol to fire a burst of gas, reciprocating the slide (just like a real gun) without actually firing a pellet at such close distances.

With training weapons so organized, we work on true close-range gunfighting drills such as close contact (weapon retention shooting), counterdraw drills, and so on. We can also begin to practice contact shooting. We are talking about being able to clash with an adversary and fire at his body from muzzle-contact distance to 10 to 18 inches away. Even a low-powered training gun like Airsoft can injure if fired this close, thus the modifications discussed.

Training at these distances truly proves the insufficiencies of techniques such as the traditional speed rock and step back and reinforces the need for integrated fighting skills. At a recent training course taught to traditional shooting school grads that had received speed rock training, I had a student stand at arm's length and gave him a rubberized training knife. I had him strike me with the knife full speed. As the knife came down, I drew into a speed rock (perhaps 1.2 seconds for a pair of gas-only shots). It was just as they'd done on the range, but the simultaneous slash across my jugular with the training knife, and the bad guy knocking me back onto the mat, knife still in his hand, drove home the fact that it was a flawed technique. Another lightbulb. Then we showed them the close-range gunfighting (CRG) drills for spitting-distance fights.

These CRG drills are done to full completion. That is, the student responds to the antagonist's move, strikes him, shoots him to the ground, and follows up. He conducts after-action assessments, looks for cover, and so on. In short, he acts as if it's a real fight, with the result of ingraining the desired mental process under greater stress than is possible in other training venues.

Note that although there is a competitive nature to some of these drills, they are still set up with roles of good guy and bad guy assigned to each party. They are short-duration events with very little shooting going on but a great deal of moving and a great deal of learning.

LEVEL TWO: SIMPLE SCENARIOS

Once a fighter has gotten good at hitting the bag and technique drills, he needs to put those skills to the test in uncontrolled situations. Likewise, after the gunfighting trainee has developed the ability to deal with real human adversaries in the drills and knows what a man looks like in his sights, he must take those skills and play with them in less-structured scenarios. The key to success here is to keep it very simple. Instead of developing some horrendous multiple terrorist takeover/nuclear national security scenario where the trainee must do incredible things to merely live through it, we present him with a very simple situation that tests the skills learned in level one.

It is important that these scenarios be goal-directed. In other words, the first thing the students must know is what their mission is. Take a typical house-search scenario. Is the goal to rescue family members, to get out and escape, to hunt down the intruder? What is the trainee's purpose? We define that and then design a *simple* scenario around the mission objective.

One example is an unknown subject (bad guy or good guy?) approaching the student as anyone on the street, including a bad guy, might. The unknown subject can either ask for directions or reach for a weapon. There are five repetitions of the scenario, and in one of them (the student doesn't know which), the subject will attack the student with a knife or gun. So we have a degree of normal interaction without the need to act with violence, yet the preparation to act is always there.

It's important for the bad guy to stick to his assigned role and not try to outwit his training partner, lest no development take place. This is still a cooperative scenario to a degree.

This same scenario can be developed further to have three unknown threats. At the critical point, only one actually

More complex scenarios bring all prior skills into focus.

attacks the student while the others are simply onlookers, or two attack and one runs away. There's room for imagination and creativity here, but we still keep them simple, realistic, intense, and short.

LEVEL THREE: COMPLEX SCENARIOS

Complex scenarios require a greater degree of thinking and planning on the part of the student (and trainer). Such a scenario might involve a good guy defending against a home invasion, an in-progress robbery at his business, or a terrorist takeover. This entails entering into the scenario with a clear

In the more complex scenarios, vehicles and other props from everyday life can be used. The idea is to make the training as real as possible without making it unsafe.

mission, dealing with the problem presented, and accomplishing the objective.

Understand that a scenario does not necessarily need the good guy to jump in shooting. Say the scenario is a home invasion, and the good guy's mission is to get to the family safe room. He may be able to do that without firing a shot, or it may require every single shot he has. These scenarios are a test of tactical thinking as well as shooting skills.

LEVEL FOUR: INTEGRATED SCENARIOS

Level four involves blending all force options from shoot-

Integrated scenarios allow the students to experiment with various force options. Here Mr. Suarez discussed integrating OC spray with the pistol for the option of ending the hostilities with less-than-lethal force but still retaining the ability to escalate.

ing to knifing to striking to disarming the bad guy, and so on. The key issue is that all participants have a similar skill level. In other words, if the scenario will involve disarms or the use of training knives, the students (both good guys and bad guys) must be up to speed on these and know how to use them (more specifically, use them safely). The drawback is that most "gun people" don't have training in anything other than guns. That must be addressed through reality-based training.

One internationally famous trainer dismisses the practice of integrating combatives with the tired phrase "You either shoot or you fight." I suspect a one-year combatives student could grab him and choke him into unconsciousness before he could say "front sight" and walk off with his prized custom gun tucked into his jeans. This is an area that is sadly lacking. To be complete warriors, students should be able to operate (not necessarily become masters, but be able to operate) with all weapons (firearms as well as knives), with combatives, and with any other possible item.

Take the example of a student who is caught unaware in a scenario and has a gun stuck in his face. Tactically, he isn't going to outdraw the bad guy. He can only attempt a disarm because his concealed gun is not quickly accessible at such a close interval. The FOF class is not the place for a tutorial on disarming. The student should already know how. If the scenario is to be run with a knife in the good guy's possession and then allow him to transition to the adversary's gun, the students should have experience and ability in using the knife. Running integrated scenarios requires highly trained and advanced students.

LEVEL FIVE: FULL-CONTACT SCENARIOS

This is the highest level of simulation and involves full-force fighting. Safety precautions are still followed, but striking, ground fighting, throwing, and other hand-to-hand combat skills are in play, as is a bad guy who will not quit so easily. Thus the good guy has a true challenge facing him. He may experience unexpected failures to stop the adversary, a charging bad guy armed with a contact weapon, and more. He may need to resort to alternative force and strike the bad guy, or he may need to shoot him many times. This is simply a high-volume, no-holds-barred version of the integrated scenario.

There is still some control because the Airsoft pistol (or any other simulated firearm) will not elicit a ballistic effect from the one who is shot, but the scenario is done at a highly violent level. You cannot train at this level constantly, and it takes a good bit of training to be able to do it, but it does give students a realistic taste of the world of personal combat.

7

THE RANGES OF CONFLICT

The outset of a potential confrontation may involve a surprise attack, but more likely it will be preceded by an interview and examination of sorts by the bad guys. Show fear, or look like an easy mark, and they will try you.

As FOF training progresses, students learn that there are ranges to all combat. The techniques used depend largely on the range interval involved. It's no different than the interval concept in martial combatives training. The lesson here is, use the wrong technique and pay the price.

Psychological Range—No attack has been made, but the Observe and Orient phases of the Observe-Orient-Decide-Act cycle are already under way. This is where the interview takes place. The good-guy trainee's positioning with regard to his adversaries, as well as his ability to disengage, plays an active role here. This is "before the fight" country, and he may be able to move as needed and utilize cover preemptively.

This is the realm of the gun. Even at a dead run, the adversary will not be able to close on you before you get your pistol in hand and pointed at him.

This exchange, in fact, can take place at various actual distances, but for the purposes of this discussion it is listed first because it's a precombat issue.

Weapons Range—Both parties can get their weapons out without making contact with one another. This is the range where most gun training stops. In my opinion it extends from five yards out to the ballistic capability of the weapon—which in reality, with handguns, probably doesn't exceed 25 yards. It's still possible to move as needed and utilize cover. It is primarily a shooting problem.

At some point you will reach the distance at which you cannot obtain the pistol in response to an attack and must precede your draw with some form of combatives technique or dynamic movement.

Integrated Range—In the contact weapon systems this is called "long range." This distance is approximately three yards out. I could include a long discourse on what works here, but with the focus being on the gun, what's essential is that unless the bad guy is stationary and gun-focused, the good guy must preface any draw with dynamic movement and a combatives technique. I cannot emphasize enough how important it is that he move off line when he draws. If moving is essential, moving first—that is, being offside—is even more crucial.

- Think of the Teuller drill (21-foot rule). If an average guy can cover 21 feet in 1.5 seconds, how much less time will he need to cover half that distance? A thug with a contact weapon can close and cut before the good guy can get his gun out. Even if the good guy got off one shot in some sort of desperate, speed-rock-type draw, his one shot would not likely stop such a man unless it hit him in the brain.
- For those who think they can outdraw one of my students at three yards from a street-carry holster without employing a combatives technique prior to the draw, all I can say is come and try it. If you can pull it off, I'll give you $100.
- Notice that there is a "no-man's-land" between the weapons and integrated ranges (4 yards + or -) where it can go either way, depending on skills, age, size, and so on. Students training in this zone feel uncomfortable just drawing but aren't quite certain they need to use combatives first. Like many things in a fight, it's an individual call.

Combatives Range—This distance, inside of three yards, is where the two adversaries can reach out and touch each other with fingers or feet. The JKD guys might call this "kicking range." It is where most of our social interaction occurs. Here it is mandatory to strike with a palm or fist prior to drawing, or the bad guy can easily forestall and/or derail the

Examine each distance interval as it appears from your perspective. Could you draw? Could you move off line? Would you need an integration of force or combatives?

good guy's draw. The closer the good guy is to his adversary, the more proactive and preemptive he must be. This is the realm of things like preemptive defensive strikes and close-contact shooting. If a knife man moves first here, the good guy will very likely be cut unless he has some reflexive defensive skills on board . . . and even then, there are no guarantees.

I must point out that this is aggressive shooting. A man who waits for an attack to physically materialize at this range will be hit by it long before he can respond. Again, I don't expect students to take my word for it. They need to do it force-on-force and see for themselves.

Clinch Range—Another term for this interval might be gun grappling range, but standing up. This is where the good-guy trainee needs to fight for his gun and retain it, manhandle the other man into a position for a contact shot, and/or employ alternative force. The gun is generally not the first option because he cannot get to it in time. Remember, we are not training with ceremonial range holsters but street gear!

Ground Fighting—This is not the place to be. The trainee may find himself here, but it is definitely not Plan A. His goal is to get back on his feet ASAP. Contact shots, ground gun grappling, and knives to the throat are the order of the day. This is no time to be squeamish about biting off ears and gouging eyes. When this happens, all bets are off; all laws are postponed. It's attack, attack, attack!

When training at these ranges, it's important for students to have a go-between—a referee of sorts—to make certain that no one gets carried away, figuratively and literally.

NECESSARY SAFETY PRECAUTIONS

There are safety measures that must be taken to ensure safe and profitable training. Students must have a full face mask as well as long sleeves and gloves. It's also critical that they be certain that the training weapons they are using are safe.

FOF training pushes the envelope of safety. Is it dangerous? Not as dangerous as conducting shoot house exercises with live firearms. With properly organized training, no one will get killed in FOF. (I say "properly organized" because there are cases of scenarios being run with one of those "police-only" simulation systems that ended with students being killed by other students when real guns were brought into the training scenario, or when real ammo was mixed with the simulated ammo.) Nonetheless, FOF is not your typical lazy Sunday afternoon shooting session. Students will get a little bruised and banged, they will get pushed around, and they will safely learn about true gunfighting. I think its essential training, but it's not for everyone. Students must adhere to the following rules to ensure that FOF training is as safe as possible.

SAFETY RULES

- No weapons of any type will be allowed in the training environment. They will be placed in a location designated by the instructor and not touched until the training day is over. No exceptions. Anyone who can't abide by that should stay home.
- Students will obey instructions. If they are told to fall down when shot, they must do it. Safety depends on everyone following instructions. FOF is a cooperative event designed to create a learning environment. Anyone who is not prepared for this should stay home.
- Everyone will wear eye protection in the form of an approved facemask, long-sleeved shirt, and gloves during pellet and gas training. Although the gloves and the long sleeves can be set aside for gas-only scenarios, facemasks are still required.
- All training weapons (Airsoft, rubber knives, etc.) will be considered real weapons and handled as such. Students cannot become lax with weapon handling in FOF. They must treat training weapons as if they are the real deal.

9

AIRSOFT AND OTHER NECESSARY GEAR

An Airsoft Glock 19. It is identical in weight and handling to an actual firearm, but it is perfectly safe to use for interactive training.

What does the individual student need to get started with FOF training? First of all, he will need a place to train. While training with Airsoft pistols does not require a special place in the traditional sense of a shooting range and can be done anywhere, the student will need some security. He can't have family members walking into his training session and getting hit in the eye with a pellet.

My suggestion is that students follow the same safety guidelines that they do when conducting dry-fire drills. The training site must be isolated and private so that the student will not be disturbed or distracted during his session and so that no uninvolved parties can get in.

There's no reason to limit training to FOF material. Students can set up their training so that they are doing square-range drills against an actual cardboard target with

The Airsoft gun is seen next to an actual Glock 23. Aside from the red markings at the muzzle of the training gun, the two are virtually identical.

Paintball/Airsoft mask and balaclava seen on a training dummy.

their Airsoft. Many of my students who live in areas with extreme climates may be away from a shooting range for three months out of the year. They use Airsoft to keep up their skills. The greatest benefit, of course, will be realized in FOF drills, but either way, the same concerns exist.

It's essential to have privacy and security in the training site. It can be a private office, a home, or even a warehouse. There should be nothing in the line of fire or anticipated impact zone that could be broken or damaged by training activities. Airsoft will not damage things like other simulated training guns will, but I would not want to hit my wife's favorite vase with a three-round burst to test it.

Personal training gear is another requirement. Let's look at safety gear first. (Obviously, this is only for FOF; no safety gear is needed for simple range exercises done with Airsoft.) Protection for eyes and face is needed for FOF. It's also a good idea to protect the arms and hands, since they tend to get hit often. A full day of FOF will take its toll on bare hands and arms and can draw blood. The same goes for bare legs.

In addition to an Airsoft pistol and accompanying equipment, I suggest the following gear, all of which is required in my own FOF classes:

Paintball/Airsoft Mask—This is a simple mask used by paintball players that will protect the face and eyes from impact and injury.

A Balaclava with a Bib—This is the kind used by spec-ops teams to prevent flash burns. We use it to protect the bare skin of the head (especially for those of us with less hair than we once had), and the lower portion of the balaclava will protect the neck area.

Long-Sleeved Sweatshirt—This keeps the close-interval shots from impacting on bare skin. Close shots from an Airsoft can break unprotected skin and are quite painful.

Gloves to Protect the Hands—These gloves must not impede the operation of the weapon. I use my old Nomex gloves from my SWAT days.

Along with this stuff, it's important to wear long pants, such as jeans, to protect the legs. That is all the protection that is required. The protective equipment listed here will offer protection from the Airsoft pellets, but the trainee will still have an immediate recognition of being hit.

Finally, it's important that anyone involved in FOF training, whether as participants or as observers, wear similar safety equipment.

LINE DRILLS—
FORCE-ON-
FORCE BASICS

These students go through basic line drills to familiarize themselves with actual street confrontation dynamics.

When a student of combatives is learning to fight, line drills, or one-step sparring, are an important part of training. Line drills fill the gap between hitting the bag and actual combat sparring. They allow the trainees to face each other, adopting roles of attacker and defender. The attacker will attack with some type of punch or kick. The defender will counter with a predetermined technique and carry it to conclusion. Although line drills are a far cry from the chaos of pure combat, they allow the trainees to develop the attributes of balance and decreased reaction time and to learn how to maneuver and operate around a human adversary.

In the study of gunfighting, we can use similar methodology, with the help of Airsoft pistols to replicate the dynamics of close-range gunfighting. These gunfighting line drills allow students to execute every training drill done on the firing range against a *human* training partner. These line drills accomplish a number of things. They teach the student what a human adversary looks like in front of his gun muzzle and about the difficulties and problems associated with hitting a 3D aggressor. They teach him the relationship between time and distance. And they teach him something about the dynamics of conflict and the reality of how easy it is to get hurt in an actual fight.

The line drills are divided into gas-only drills and gas and pellet drills. Gas-only drills are designed for ultraclose-quarters drills where the pistol would be fired at contact distances to the adversary. The Airsoft guns are temporarily modified by taping down the slide lock levers with duct tape. This allows the magazine to be loaded with gas but not with pellets. The guns will then function just as they would when actually firing a pellet but will expel only gas from the muzzle. In spite of this temporary modification, the slides on the guns will still reciprocate back and forth just like a real firearm would when fired. This allows students to work drills in close proximity to training partners and gain the benefit of experiencing the simulated firing of the weapon in such proximity without excessive impact on training partners.

Gas and pellet drills do without the modifications employed for gas-only drills, allowing students to actually shoot at each other with pellets. Gas and pellet drills should be reserved for distances of five yards and beyond.

GAS-ONLY DRILLS

Gunfighting Line Drill 1—This drill involves gas only and is done at five yards. Two trainees face each other armed with Airsoft gas-only pistols. One is given the role of aggressor and the other the role of defender. The aggressor begins the drill by reaching for his weapon. (This is to give the defender the visual cue to draw, as opposed to an audible cue on the firing range.) The defender sees this overt action and responds by moving off line quickly as he draws his own weapon and "shoots" the aggressor multiple times. The drill is stopped immediately at this point and then repeated several times before the roles are reversed. The drill should be repeated with the aggressor at 9:00, 3:00, and 6:00.

Gunfighting Line Drill 2—The drill above is repeated, but at a closer distance interval. The students face each other at 2.5 yards, and the same exchange takes place. The students will learn that as the distance decreases, the time to react also decreases and the movement off line on the draw must be more dynamic. The drill should be repeated with the aggressor at 9:00, 3:00, and 6:00.

Gunfighting Line Drill 3—This distance expansion drill begins to expose the trainee to true close-range combat. The trainees face each other as aggressor and defender. The aggressor reaches for his belt in an attempt get a weapon. The defender sees the overt attempt and gives him a palm strike to the face (high five). Be careful with this drill so that no injury takes place. As the strike is delivered and the hand begins to recoil, the defender drops his foot back, taking two steps backward in a natural manner. As this is taking place, he draws and fires a group of shots into the aggressor. The defender may add a shot to the face as well, in anticipation of a failure to stop. The drill is stopped immediately at this point and then repeated several times before the roles are reversed. The drill should be repeated with the aggressor at 9:00, 3:00, and 6:00.

Gunfighting Line Drill 4—This distance-compression drill is the same basic drill, but in this case the objective is to drive into and through the aggressor, and not to create distance or get away. There are times when "getting in his face" makes more tactical sense than getting away. The trainees face each other as aggressor and defender. The aggressor reaches for his belt in an attempt get a weapon. The defender sees the overt attempt and gives him a palm strike to the face. As the strike is delivered, the trainee drives forward into and through the aggressor, stepping forward two steps. As this is taking place, he draws and fires a group of shots into the aggressor's body and face. The aggressor should end up on his back on the ground. The drill is stopped immediately at this point and then repeated several times before the roles are reversed. The drill should be repeated with the aggressor at 9:00, 3:00, and 6:00.

GAS AND PELLET DRILLS

Gunfighting Line Drill 5—This drill is conducted at seven yards. The aggressor is armed with a large, padded full-contact training knife. The defender is armed with an Airsoft

Gunfighting Line Drill 5 can get very exciting if the attacking knife man can close faster than the student can get off the line of attack.

A student is able to evade his attackers and respond with simulated gunfire during Line Drill 6.

pistol (gas and pellet). Both trainees are armored. The aggressor begins the drill by charging the defender with the intent of slapping him across the face with the training knife. The defender must recognize the oncoming attack, move quickly and dynamically off line, and get his gun out and working. The drill is stopped immediately at this point. It can be repeated with the aggressor coming from different angles as well.

Gunfighting Line Drill 6—The previous drill is repeated, but this time with the other students surrounding the pair in a large circle. Immediately upon neutralizing the aggressor, the defender begins his after-action assessment, making certain the aggressor is down, looking for another hostile, looking behind him, and so on. There is another unknown aggressor in the crowd. If the defender fails to be watchful and remain on guard, the second aggressor must attack him with full intent. To control the evolution of the drill and keep it from degrading into an uncontrolled "hose-down," the num-

Gunfighting Line Drill 7 simulates a street fight where both combatants are armed with pistols. This teaches students the importance of speed and movement as well as the dynamics of reaction time.

ber of pellets given to the defender for his gun is held to approximately six.

Gunfighting Line Drill 7—This drill is conducted at five yards. Both the aggressor and the defender are armed with Airsoft pistols (gas and pellet). Both trainees are armored. The aggressor begins the drill by attempting to draw his weapon and fire. The defender must recognize the oncoming attack, move quickly and dynamically off line, and get his gun out and working. The drill is stopped immediately at this point. It can be repeated with the aggressor coming from different angles as well.

Gunfighting Line Drill 8—The drill above is repeated, but this time with the other students surrounding the pair in a large circle. Immediately upon neutralizing the aggressor,

When dealing with multiple adversaries, the rule of the day is move faster than they do, move first, and take the initiative. Reactive shooters get shot by multiple adversaries.

the defender begins his after-action assessment, making certain the aggressor is down, looking for another hostile, looking behind him, and so on. There is another unknown aggressor in the crowd. If the defender fails to be watchful and remain on guard, the second aggressor must attack him with full intent. To limit the drill and prevent it from degenerating into a game, the number of pellets given to the defender for his gun is held to approximately six.

Gunfighting Line Drill 9—The trainee/defender faces three aggressors at seven yards. They are all armed with gas and pellet pistols. On *go* the defender attempts to move quickly off line and shoot each one of the aggressors. Simultaneously, the aggressors attempt to shoot the defender. Often, the defender will get shot because he hesitates; that is, instead of acting, he reacts to the actions of his adversaries. This is one of the only

These photos depict gunfight simulations against multiple attackers. Once a student understands the dynamics of movement and reaction time, the danger of such a situation is greatly reduced.

drills where the trainee learns more from failing than from succeeding. It will teach him that when facing greater forces, the only viable solution in a fight is to attack without waiting; in other words, the best way to survive is to start the fight, or be offsides, as we say.

Gunfighting Line Drill 10—This is the same as the previous drill except for one thing: instead of everyone moving on *go*, the trainee defender gets to start the fight. He will move off line and begin shooting the aggressors as soon as he wishes, forcing them to react to him. The drill can be set up with the aggressors spread out in a line, a tight group, or any configuration imaginable. Initially, however, to make the mental connection between firing range and FOF, it's best to line them up for inspection just like in the drills on the range.

These are only a few drills designed to replicate the typical square-range training drills conducted at nearly every shooting school in the nation. Similar drills can be developed and organized based on other firing drills not mentioned. The important thing to remember with line drills is that they must be kept simple and direct. The human aggressors have in essence taken the place of the paper target.

SIMPLE SCENARIO DRILLS— FORCE-ON-FORCE APPLICATIONS

The simple scenario can be applied to any level of students. It is short, intense, and imparts an important lesson. Here Mr. Suarez briefs a counterterrorist group in Spain.

Once students have been through gunfighting line drills and understand the lessons they teach, it is time for simple scenarios. Simple scenarios are different from the line drills in that they are not "set up;" that is, they are less structured. Simple scenarios are not the elaborate and ambitious single-handed, 12-magazine invasions of terrorist strongholds often seen at entertainment-based shooting schools. Rather, they are portions of real-life events reenacted for training purposes.

The simple scenarios are not codified as the line drills are. They can be written, organized, and developed in custom manner, depending on the information that is accessible. Here are some examples:

You can involve the use of automobiles to an extent previously impossible with live fire. Here a student deploys and responds to a carjacking scenario.

Carjacking—The defender is standing at the driver's-side door of a car when the aggressor approaches him. The aggressor may or may not necessarily mount an attack. He may simply ask for directions, or he may produce a knife and attempt to plunge it into the defender's chest. This is a very simple scenario based on an event that's common in daily life, i.e., being approached by an unknown individual of unknown intent.

The key is to be ready without overreacting. Suggestions for correct procedure include being alert and refusing to allow the unknown person to approach without taking some postural measures (in other words, face the threat—do not let him approach from your flank). Eye contact and an unwel-

Home invasions, takeover robberies, and active shooter incidents can all be replicated in a business space.

coming "what do you want" make a good opening, all the while remaining suspicious of his intent and prepared should it be a sinister one. If an attack is initiated, the defender meets it with the correct response learned in the line drills. If no attack is forthcoming, then the defender deals with the potential threat and continues on his way. It's important that the attack not *always* come. If there are three repetitions of the scenario, one will be an attack and the other two will not be. The scenario can be made more complex, but it is best to save that for later.

Home Invasion—Again, this is a simple segment of a complex problem. The defender is either sitting or lying down in a simulated bed. He may be reading the newspaper out loud. Suddenly, two men burst through a door and move toward him without warning, armed with contact weapons. (It's important that the scenario be survivable. If the two aggressors burst in and shoot the defender unannounced and without warning, there is no point to the event.) The defender must locate and deploy his pistol, take cover, shoot back, do whatever is available to him at the time. After the initial confrontation, the action is stopped and the participants debriefed.

Terrorist Takeover—This is a multiple-adversary situation wherein real people are simulating a likely event. The defender is positioned among other classmates as a client in a business. He is the only one with a pistol. The other students are unarmed. Suddenly, two or more terrorists burst into the room and attempt to control everyone and herd them into a back room. The defender picks his moment and proactively attacks them with gunfire.

Again, after the initial confrontation, the action is stopped and the participants debriefed. Likewise, if the defender does not act in a timely manner, the action is stopped and the participants debriefed. Is important to realize that acting at the moment of contact may or may not be a wise tactic on the part of the defender. The wisdom of such action depends on many factors. At the same time, it is foolish for the defender to think that he will be safer if he allows himself to be taken into the back room, searched, and tied up.

Street Mugging—The defender is standing at a simulated phone booth when approached by the aggressor. The aggressor threatens with a weapon, and the defender reacts as needed to win the confrontation.

These scenarios can be elaborated upon later, but at this stage simplicity is essential to developing a quick solution and conducting a quick debriefing, which is where the learning actually occurs. Trainers and trainees alike can use their imaginations to set up and deal with these problems.

COMPLEX SCENARIO DRILLS

Complex scenarios bring all of the prior skills together, whether the student is a civilian home defender or a member of a SWAT unit with counterterrorist capabilities.

The gunfighting line drills teach the student about bridging the gap between the range and the world. The simple scenario drills take him further and show the dynamics and violence of true gunfighting. The complex scenarios now make him think and develop tactical plans.

Before students get very deep into complex scenario drills, it is essential that they be familiar with tactical principles. In the absence of such understanding, we have a well-trained marksman and fighter but not a tactical thinker. It's important to develop the warrior's mind as well as his trigger finger and aggressive nature. Thus, this chapter is a primer for understanding tactical principles as they apply to the single individual. I suggest everyone study it thoroughly and gain a working understanding before proceeding. It would also be useful to read *The Tactical Advantage* (Paladin Press, 1998).

The complex scenario differs from the simple scenario in two ways. First, it takes longer and is more difficult to implement. In a large class the complex scenarios may create some downtime as students wait their turn to role-play. Secondly, the complex scenario involves some "backstory" (a term borrowed from the movie industry to describe a method whereby a great deal of past history is communicated in a single scene). For the trainee, this demands being observant but also understanding and accepting one's first impressions of an unfolding event.

The complex scenario can also incorporate other variables such as noise, low light, and other environmental factors that the trainee cannot control. There may be role-players who give him vital information about what he is to face, such as the number of adversaries, their armament and location, and so on.

In the past, trainers with little or no operational experience would often design such scenarios as almost impossible to survive, without involving much more imagination than putting a number of bad guys into a room to ambush the unsuspecting, soon-to-die good guy. In my humble opinion, such events are a waste of time and prepare the trainee for failure. If you take any of the international gun gurus, or tactical shooting champions, or even the highest trained spec-ops soldier in the United Sates and place them in a situation such as I've described, they will get shot just like anyone else. If five well-armed and trained bad guys are hidden in a dark room, fully intent on shooting you the moment you enter, and are alert and specifically waiting for you, what do you think would happen? And furthermore, is such an event likely? And even if it were and you didn't need to go in, would you? Get the picture?

Keeping it real is essential! Not only must the scenario be a realistic simulation, but the trainee must go into it with a realistic attitude. The concepts that follow will help everyone do just that.

1) **Know your mission.** First of all, the trainee must know his mission and objective. Nobody moves into a tactical problem without having a mission. Why is he there, and what is he trying to accomplish? It is essential that these issues be addressed before the scenario begins. If there is doubt about that, then a sit-down session with the students may be in order to establish what they are prepared to do and why it may or may not be a good idea. These are tactical issues relating to objectives. Exactly *why* someone is moving through a scenario is an essential aspect of *how* he will do it. For instance, what should a single person living alone do if awakened in the middle of the night by glass breaking downstairs? How would that change for the family man who has relatives living in adjacent rooms? What if that sound came from one of the children's rooms? What if it was followed by a strange male voice? Get the idea? The trainee must not just think, "Oh, a bump in the night, let me go on the hunt." He must know what he is attempting to do.

2) **Understand that there are no guarantees.** Tactics is an art and not a science. It is the art of minimizing danger while you approach it. It is the art of killing without getting killed, pure and simple. As such, it lives in dangerous waters. A tactician might do everything correctly and still be shot by the adversary. There are no guarantees here. The trainee must recognize and accept that it is dangerous, and he may get killed while operating in this realm.

3) **Maintain situational awareness.** The best way to define situational awareness is a state of being alert. The trainee must keep his eyes open and try to see dangers before he is upon them. The most seemingly minor thing may be a big deal. What I am referring to

is *target indicators*. These are the little things that most nonwarriors dismiss as inconsequential: the muddy footprints across your rug, the door that was closed and is now open, the smell of stale cigarette smoke, the sound of breathing, all of them innocent when viewed in isolation but potentially indicative of danger when seen in the context of a tactical event. The trainee must notice them, accept them as potentially important intelligence, and use them to his benefit!

4) **Be stealthy**. Up to the point of contact, the trainee must avoid producing target indicators himself. He must avoid making unnecessary noise. He will not shine his flashlight around if there is enough light to see. He will not have a shiny gun. He is quiet. Anyone who has ever hunted knows what I mean. In fact, hunting is an excellent exercise for tactical development. The idea is to *be the hunter*.

5) **Do not assume; verify**. The trainee must not take things for granted. He must make sure his gun truly is loaded, make sure his gear works, make sure that door is in fact locked, make sure there is no one hiding behind the counter before he turns his back on it, and make sure the suspicious guy's hands truly are empty. He must make sure of everything and assume nothing!

6) **Control the distance**. Distance is a factor in the fight, or tactical problem. Nothing more and nothing less. One common mistake made by students who have only trained on 180-degree, two-dimensional ranges is that since they cannot (or are not permitted to) drive through their targets, or maneuver around them, they always rely on backpedaling, or dropping back. Big mistake, as there is a time and a place for everything. The key here is, don't expand the distance—control it.

When searching or moving through a scenario, the trainee must project ahead to upcoming danger areas. If there are no mitigating circumstances, maximizing the distance to the potential threats may be called for. The same goes for contacting potential hostiles. But the trainee should understand that there may be features of the problem that are outside his control that demand that he close in on a threat or a danger area. He must accept this and be prepared to do so.

7) **Move and act deliberately**. If the trainee knows what his mission is and his tactical wisdom has allowed him to develop a rough plan of how to get there, he must act decisively. He cannot be tentative or hesitant. If he needs to take the corner, he takes it, and he does so aggressively and decisively. This does not mean he acts carelessly or recklessly. Often we see guys simply run into a problem that could have been solved more safely, or we see guys hang around a door that they simply needed to walk through.

As far as movement, the best advice for trainees is to keep your balance at all costs and move naturally.

8) **Remember the basics on contact**. Close-quarters battle (CQB) shooting is different than the marksmanship practiced on the competitive range. The FOF trainee may not get a perfect shot. He may not get a perfect sight picture. He must learn what is required to hit a man at room distances because those are the distances of battle. It is unlikely that one would have to shoot a home invader at 50 yards. It's possible, but odds are it will happen at 5 feet. The basic principles of CQB, specifically speed, surprise, and violence, are critical.

In these scenarios, whatever the trainee does, he does it fast. There is no time to second-guess, hesitate, or evaluate. At the point of contact, the aggressor's hands and what they are holding/doing determine whether the defender shoots or not. He must recognize this quickly.

The defender learns to use the element of surprise in these scenarios. The lesson here is this: If you can ambush, bushwhack, or otherwise take your adversary unawares, do it! The best gunfight is the one where you are the only one who does any shooting. It's not fair, it's not nice; in fact, it is downright cheating. Cheat.

Too many trainers make a big deal about so-called verbalizing. They want the trainee to give orders and communicate with the man who has broken into his home intending to kill his family. Fools! The only time a verbal exchange is required is when the defender is uncertain about whether he is facing a true threat or a possible threat. He does so from a position of advantage, behind cover, not out in the open. The decision will depend on what the man in question has in his hands and what the overall situation is. Needless to say, a stranger in your home with a large knife in his hands is not a person you need say anything to. If the law requires you to do so, then adapt and overcome. Bottom line, there is no room in these scenarios for fighting fair and giving the adversary a noble chance.

All of these principles are considered and incorporated when designing complex training scenarios that are based on the realities of life in the 21st century. Following are some suggested themes:

Scenario: Home Invasion/Kidnap Attempt
- Dynamics: Three bad guys break in to capture you and your family.
- Objective: Hold them off with gunfire while your family gets to a safe area.

Scenario: Home Invasion/Night Burglary
- Dynamics: Bad guy breaks in to steal stuff. You hear him.
- Objective: Move from your bedroom to kid's bedroom to secure family.

Scenario: Takeover Robbery
- Dynamics: Two bad guys enter your place of business and threaten you and your employees.
- Objective: Feign compliance and shoot them.

Scenario: Terrorist Bomb Threat
- Dynamics: Terrorist enters business, shows bomb, and announces he will blow himself up.
- Objective: Take him out with a head shot.

Scenario: School Shooting
- Dynamics: You go to pick up kids at school and hear shooting inside. Your kids are inside.
- Objective: Move to the shooter covertly and ambush him.

The scenarios are, of course, suggested possibilities, as are the solutions. The potential missions one might have in the scenarios are variable as well. The scenarios can be run in pairs and in teams of three to make it more interesting. Some might argue about the aggressiveness of some of the objectives given in these examples. Well, that is up to the discretion of the individual creating the scenarios, but I would question the heart of a man who would hide under the bed when there is an armed man stalking his family, or allow a man to detonate a bomb when he could prevent it, or wait in the car for the SWAT team to arrive when his kids where inside a building being shot up by a psycho. There may be others who advocate running off to seek help, but in my book, *you are the help*. FOF is not for cowards, liberals, or the faint of heart.

INTEGRATED
SCENARIOS

It is likely that a confrontation will take place at an extremely close interval, and the integration of combatives may be necessary to prevent a disarm attempt . . .

. . . or to perpetuate a disarm of your adversary if doing so would be faster than drawing your own gun.

The integrated scenario is an outgrowth of the complex problems we've already discussed. The difference is that more tools are permitted. In the previous chapter, everything revolved around the Airsoft gun issued to the trainee. In the integrated scenario, the trainee may have a training knife, a second gun, a flashlight for low light, an inert canister of OC, or something else. The scenario might involve improvised weapons to thwart a terrorist on an airplane, or it may involve using a Spyderco training knife to thwart the active shooter with a throat cut.

It is essential that everyone in the scenario be briefed as to what is in play and that everyone is up to the task. Moreover, although safety is important and should be emphasized throughout, the proximity inherent to these integrated events could lead into a combatives conclusion. That is not a big deal as long as everyone understands it and recognizes that there is a limit line that will not be crossed. A predetermined signal from the trainer maybe in order to stop things if they begin to get off-topic. A good whistle is not a bad idea.

Full padded opponent suits are among the equipment that can enhance this type of training session. The suits will act as body armor for the aggressors, protecting them from the Airsoft pellets better than a simple sweatshirt can, and will also protect them from injury resulting from strikes and other impacts from the good-guy defender.

14

FULL-CONTACT SCENARIOS

A full-contact scenario involves physical contact made by both parties. It gets very real, and grads of this type and level of training are well prepared for street confrontations, regardless of the distance at which they occur.

As students of FOF training progress through the scenarios, their competitive spirits will eventually make them want to see if they can increase the volume, so to speak. The full-contact scenario allows for this.

The main problem with *any* firearm simulation training tool is that there is no reaction from the individual who gets shot (i.e., no terminal ballistics). Whereas five shots to the body plus three shots to the face from a 9mm pistol *will* elicit a terminal ballistics response from a real threat on the street, that same fusillade from an Airsoft gun to a bad-guy trainee wearing a padded sweatshirt and an Airsoft mask will not. Since people react when shot with real bullets but do not react when shot with simulated ammo, the terminal

The Teuller drill can be replicated in the full-contact scenario as well and may begin at an interval much closer than the standard seven yards.

ballistics reaction must be introduced to the scenario artificially via the bad guy's role-playing. If that reaction was not there, the good guy and bad guy would simply keep shooting at each other until they ran out of ammo, or one of the parties would blast through the pellets (that he knows will not kill him) with sheer force of will to get at his adversary. A well-trained gunfighter will shoot such an adversary to the ground with multiple gunshots to the body and head. One day I suspect we may have the technology to "stun" adversaries in the training environment sufficiently to declare a true winner and a true loser, but that technology is not yet available. As such, the bad guy's scripted response to being hit is indispensable.

These full-contact scenarios can be run in two ways. We have done them in other countries where the civil liability issues are not a concern and the participants are all trained fighters and high-speed operators in their own right. In such cases we use minimal protection (in one class we used nothing but Oakleys for eye protection), and trainees go full force when it comes to contact distances where shooting and combatives blend. The second way to run these scenarios is to armor up in the Red Man/FIST-type suits so real-time, full-force blows can be exchanged.

I seriously do not recommend this type of training unless trainees are truly ready for it. It is not for everyone, and I only mention it because we *have* done it in the past. It is analogous to the full-contact stick fights of the southern California-based Dog Brothers; injuries are not uncommon.

15

USING COVER

Cover is great if you have it, but often it is not available at the outset of a fight.

In a nutshell, cover is anything solid that offers ballistic protection. That means defenders can hide behind cover and be reasonably certain that bullets fired at it will not penetrate through and hit them. The requirement to use cover may be problematic depending on the type of armaments the adversaries have on hand. Some things that are suitable cover against a pistol may not do well as cover against a rifle.

Concealment, on the other hand, is anything that hides a defender's presence from the adversary. A good example of cover is a brick wall. A good example of concealment is darkness. Brick walls will stop most small-arms ordnance. Darkness will allow concealment, but it will not stop anything. Sometimes cover will also offer concealment, but not the other way around.

Cover may be used during a fight to avoid being shot. Concealment, on the other hand, may only be used prior to the fight to deceive the adversary as to one's whereabouts. Concealment will provide a base from which to launch an ambush. Concealment demands stealth. Sometimes that will be enough. If the opponent doesn't know the good guy is there, he won't think of shooting at him. Cover often offers the same advantages as concealment but with additional ballistic protection.

To use concealment the defender must have prior knowledge of an enemy's approach, as well as the belief that the enemy hasn't seen him. Obviously, if the enemy knows the good guy is there, hiding in the shadows will not help. To use cover effectively, a defender must have the time and room to reach it, as well as specific anticipation of hostilities.

There has been controversy about the propriety of always running to cover when a fight begins. Generally, the closer the fight is, the less time is available to respond to a threat. Defenders are often forced to react and solve the problem with gunfire before even considering cover. The proximity and duration of most urban gunfights are important to bear in mind. They are low-duration, high-intensity fights. If the defender is attacked, his response must be to counterattack immediately.

Sure, the argument that you can fight back *while* running to cover exists. But stop reading for a moment and consider something: right now, where you are, where is cover, and can you get to it? Consider, too, that the human mind cannot focus on too many things at a time in stressful situations.

In more than half a dozen combat situations I've been engaged in, cover was not a factor for me. Only after the initial shots were fired and returned did it even occur to anyone to look for cover. Our gunfire *was* our cover.

Sometimes, however, the gunfire may come from an unknown area, or from such a long distance that it precludes an instant counterattack. At such times, moving to cover first is a good idea. A good rule of thumb is that if you do not have a target to shoot at when you come under fire, *get behind cover.*

It's important to realize that many things most people consider as cover are really only concealment. In some tactical simulations, the environments are very artificial, using cardboard walls and furniture that give the illusion of cover with no ballistic protection and incorporating items intended to replicate things that can be used as cover in the real world. Rule of thumb: if it doesn't stop bullets, it's not cover. When in doubt, shoot it and see if the bullets go through. Most of the things people tend to hide behind with the idea they are taking cover (e.g., furniture, trash cans, and mailboxes) are easily penetrated by gunfire.

The same goes for corners and walls inside buildings, as well as doors. Most modern cartridges will penetrate directly through these light wood and stucco structures. Therefore, if an adversary fires from a doorway, the good guy can shoot him right through the wall! Even buckshot will work in such situations.

Automobiles, on the other hand, make relatively good cover against most small-arms fire, except for centerfire rifle fire. The exception here is the side window glass, which is as resistive to gunfire as a piece of paper.

The defender should seek as hard a point of cover as possible but realize that such hard cover will tend to cause projectiles to ricochet. Bullets often tend to ricochet along a parallel axis to the cover they've struck and angled slightly away from it. If the defender is too close to his cover, they'll ricochet right into him. The magic distance seems to be at least six feet. By staying at least this distance from his cover, the defender can rest assured that the ricochet's angle of departure will have grown enough to bypass him completely. Again, *if the defender crowds his cover, he runs the risk of getting hit with a ricochet.*

Remember when I said that there are no absolutes to tactics, and that tactics is an art, not a science? Remember when I said we would revisit this later? There are times when getting closer to cover than the prescribed six-foot distance makes sense. One such time is when the adversary is shooting from above, such as from a second-story window. If the good guy moves too far from his cover, the adversary will be able to bypass that cover by virtue of his higher position and shoot down into the good guy's position. Yes, by moving closer the good guy may run a greater risk of ricochets, but he runs a greater risk of getting shot outright the other way. Additionally, if he is engaging multiple adversaries at different points, he must be cognizant of the possibility that they may pinpoint him and attempt to flank his position. So he must note his adversaries' locations and stay alert!

In Interactive Gunfighting/FOF training we discuss the use of cover but realize from personal experience that it will probably *not* be a readily available option at the outset of a fight. Our courses go far beyond the simple scenario of "go find the bad guy in the shoot house." We don't take range drills and force them to work in a more dynamic environment; rather, we teach our students how to fight with their guns in as realistic an environment as possible while still ensuring that training progresses in a safe manner for everyone involved.

16

STAPLE OF TACTICAL MOVEMENT— ANGULAR SEARCH

Understanding the angular search concept as applied to a corner enables the tactical shooter to maneuver through any tactical problem.

If a marksmanship instructor can boil everything down to aligning the sights and pressing the trigger, then a tactics instructor can take everything related to searching and/or moving through a building and boil it down to the angular search. Also known as cornering or pieing, this type of maneuver offers a way to negotiate a corner safely at any speed and any angle. The student who learns it well will understand tactics. The angular search is best learned by using it on a corner. Any tactical environment can be viewed as a series of corners. A hallway is an avenue with many corners. "T" intersections and doorways are combinations of double corners. Even a stairway is nothing more than a set of horizontal and vertical corners.

The angular search is based on mind-set. One must not go about cornering with a lack of purpose or a tentative attitude.

It's essential to "get your mind right," as my old field training officer (FTO) used to say. A gunfight is a violent and aggressive event, so the warrior in training must get aggressive in his mind and heart. This does not mean reckless, but neither does it mean fearful or hesitant. A good warrior tactician knows what his plan is and why it must be accomplished.

The warrior must stay alert and calm and not allow himself to be startled at anything he may encounter. He must be mentally prepared for any eventuality, accepting and assessing the scene and environment before him. He will evaluate what he sees as he is moving. He will eliminate the locations where the adversary/danger is not, so that he can focus on the more likely locations. There is no way to tentatively take a corner. It's important to adopt the attitude that every step taken is pressing the adversary to a point of no return.

The warrior cannot wait until the last moment before beginning his angular movement. He must commence cornering as soon as he can. The more distance he places between himself and the corner, the better for him in most cases. Once he is boxed in, right on top of the corner, his ability to assess and support his movements with his weapon is drastically reduced.

He cannot be afraid to move as necessary in order to see whatever he needs to see of the corner. He will move up or down, change ready positions, change the weapon hand, even give ground momentarily if necessary. And he must try to see as much of the unsecured space beyond the corner as possible before committing to it.

He must be sure that he does not drag his feet, scrape his clothing on the wall, or flatten against the wall as he approaches. Stealth is his best friend at this time. He must avoid anything that might alert the adversary who is potentially beyond the corner to his presence. He must avoid standing too close to the wall, not only because incoming rounds may ricochet into him but also because doing so limits his movement options.

When he begins approaching the corner, he must see the

The same concept of clearing/moving is used by virtually all of the high-speed tactical teams in the world.

The closer you get to the point of the corner, the more alert you must be.

apex of the corner as a pivot point for his movement. He varies the height, speed, and angle of his approach as needed. Foremost in his mind is that he is hunting a man and that man is hunting him. Therefore, he will not be where his adversary expects him to be. Some schools advocate taking corners from kneeling and/or prone. I generally advocate trying to remain standing as much as possible. Mobility and stealth are the tactical shooter's best friends here; it's unwise for him to turn his back on them by going prone.

As the trainee approaches the apex of the corner, he will move away from it in a semicircle as if he is tethered to the corner itself. This is the action that gave cornering the name "slicing the pie." As he moves forward along that half circle,

Briskly!

tied to that imaginary tether, he will scan the area ahead "a slice at a time." Eventually, he reaches a point of commitment where he has scanned as much as he can and any further forward movement may expose him to the adversary. This is the point of no return, which is breaking into and taking that unsecured space.

Now let's pause for just a moment. When the tactical shooter steps off into the unknown and takes that unsecured space, he may come face-to-face with an armed enemy ready and willing to kill him. He must be prepared to shoot immediately as he moves into that space. The decision should be based on an assessment of the overall situation, but specifically he is looking for weapons in the hands and/or aggressive action. He cannot take this lightly. He must always remember that, all things being equal, he has one chance in three: 1) the adversary shoots him, 2) he shoots the adversary, or 3) they shoot each other.

So the trainee must move briskly, but under control. He will visually locate and immediately evaluate the man on the other side. If there is a weapon, he will shoot while he moves and keep moving. In FOF exercises the men who take the corner and stand there get shot. The men who take the corner on the move, shoot, and keep moving do not get shot. They avoid the desire to stand their ground and slug it out. Instead, they move and shoot to avoid being where the adversary is shooting.

The concept of the angular search is an important one to learn. It should be considered as important as the concept of seeing the front sight. It doesn't even take a firearm or an Airsoft to practice this. It's a matter of simply going into a building and looking for corners, moving through one corner and then to the next, trying to see all the corners in the environment, and considering how one would move through them both when time is of the essence and when there's all the time in the world. By doing this, FOF students will begin to develop a good tactical sense.

HOSTILE-CONTACT PROCEDURES

A man is not a two-dimensional target. How you handle this situation will dictate how the fight develops.

Invariably, while working through these scenario sessions, the trainee will end up facing a potential threat at gunpoint. He is a man of unknown intent who cannot be shot but who arouses suspicion. This is an area that is often ignored when it comes to training the private operator. Why? Because most tactical courses are designed for the policeman, or the soldier acting as policeman, whose mission is to capture the bad guy. The private citizen operator has no such requirements.

The private citizen operator (good guy) has simplicity of purpose. His job is to ensure his and his family's survival. Killing the bad guy may be the only way to ensure that he accomplishes mission one. If escape from or avoidance of the bad guy is possible, great. If not, then a confrontation must take place. If it calls for shooting, the citizen operator can accomplish that easily. If shooting is not warranted, then he must command the bad guy to do what he says immediately.

The good guy must understand that the bad guy is not afraid of his gun or his school-approved technique. If the bad guy fears anything, it will be the good guy himself. That is why the citizen operator must communicate clearly through his demeanor and attitude that he has no problem with shooting to kill and has no intention of discussing anything with the bad guy or allowing him to do anything but follow orders.

Americans are taught to be excessively nice and compliant—at least they were up until the terrorist attack of September 11, 2001. Nevertheless, the old programming lies just beneath the surface. There is no need to be rude or insulting, but the good guy must be unyielding in issuing his commands. If the bad guy fails to comply immediately, or takes a step, or does anything but what he has been ordered to do, the good guy must be prepared: he will probably have to shoot him.

The good guy cannot stand around in the open barking orders; he must get behind cover first, or he will get shot. Once he is safely behind cover, he will issue the following commands:

1) DON'T MOVE! I've used capitals to emphasize that the good guy should sound like Clint Eastwood, not Pee-wee Herman, when he says this. If the bad guy makes a wrong move, such as reaching for his belt, the good guy shoots.

2) HANDS UP! *Asking* to see his hands is a grave mistake, because he will show them, muzzle first. If he brings them up halfway, the follow-up order is "UP!"

Now here is where some prior soul-searching may be called for so the citizen operator is clear in his mind about his mission. He must decide in advance whether it is better for him and his family if he orders the bad guy to get the @#*& out of the house or holds him for the police. Again, he must determine this ahead of time so there is no hesitation when the Final Exam comes. Each situation is different, but if the bad guy goes away it may be better than keeping him at gunpoint in the house. On the other hand, he may come back. One thing is certain: unless the status of all family members is known, letting the bad guy go is not an option. I don't need to elaborate on that dynamic do I?

If the goal is to get the bad guy out of the house, the third command is simple:

3) GET OUT OF MY HOUSE OR I'LL KILL YOU WHERE YOU STAND!

Clarity is golden. If the goal is to contain him, the commands are as follows:

3) GET DOWN! GET DOWN NOW!
4) ON YOUR FACE!
5) HANDS OUT IN FRONT!
6) DON'T MOVE OR I'LL KILL YOU!

There is no place for getting all whimpery and worried about using the words "I'll kill you." The good guy must be crystal clear in what he communicates to the thug he is holding at gunpoint. If he does kill him, so what? The bad guy was doing something threatening, and he had already been warned in no uncertain terms.

A thug is not going to get the right message if the good guy is holding his pistol down by his leg to avoid violating imaginary rule two (never let the muzzle cover anything or anyone) while mumbling something about "taking appropriate action in accordance with the revised statutes of the circuit court of la-la land." Taking such a tack may, in fact, leave the good guy no choice but to shoot. On the other hand, the thug who is looking directly into muzzle while hearing a good imitation of Sgt. Rock tell him he'll be shot dead unless he does everything he's told is much more likely to comply. And if not, the good guy is in a much better position to save himself and carry out his warning.

18

LOW-LIGHT GUNFIGHTING (FORCE-ON-FORCE)

FOF training must include the aspects of reduced-light confrontation or, as I like to call it, low-light gunfighting. Most students of the gun get to do some low-light training, but it is usually limited to learning either the Harries or the Rogers flashlight technique on the range, followed by some shooting in darkness with said techniques. Period. A few others may get the option to walk through a so-called shoot house and pop two-dimensional paper targets like those they were shooting on the range. All very educational and interesting, but the same dynamics I discussed earlier are at play here. Low-light FOF will fill in the gaps left by range training alone. The complex scenario and the integrated scenario offer the best opportunities to practice and develop good low-light gunfighting skills.

Following are the basic rules of thumb for low-light gun-fighting, as taught in FOF training:

1) **Darkness is your friend**. Too many defenders wish to stand in the light, thinking that light offers safety. Not the case at all. Instead, move into the dark as soon as you have entered the low-light environment. Exposure in the light is as deadly as anything. Stay concealed. Darkness will give you that. See without being seen.

2) **Assess the available light**. When facing a tactical problem, read the varying light levels. Note the ambient light, points of darkness, and sources of light. Your reading of the light will dictate your tactics as well as your use of flashlights or other artificial assistance.

3) **Locate specific dark danger areas**. Just as you assess a room for potential danger areas in daylight, you must pick out specific points of darkness, shadowed areas behind doors, and other obstacles, as well as in corners.

4) **Ask yourself what the enemy sees**. Stop and try to see with your adversary's eyes and from his perspective. What are you exposing? Are you backlit or casting a shadow? Is your weapon reflecting light?

5) **Move and light, light and move**. Lights are targets. You may need light to see, but use it sparingly. If you use the light, turn it on from a position of advantage (cover), scan quickly, and move with it off. Use the light in erratic flashes and sweeps. Paint an area quickly to pick out where you wish to go next. Use strobing or pulsation of the light from different levels as you approach a specific point of concern. This will deny

the enemy information about your exact location. Use constant light only when you are backlit (a situation you should always seek to avoid) or when you have located and are dealing with a specific adversary that has either been neutralized or is not in a position to shoot you. Think movement every time you use the light, and understand that the light need not be on for you to fire an accurate shot and hit your adversary. Thus, you can flash the adversary with a quick burst of light and move (quickly deciding whether he needs to be shot or not), shoot him with or without another burst of the light, and move again.

You are using the darkness as well as the diminished state of the adversary's eyes (try flashing your eye with a tactical flashlight and see what I mean) to deny him a clear picture of your immediate position, but you now know where he is. Also, if he fires you will have his muzzle flash to key in on and shoot at.

6) **Be flexible with your light**. Do not get locked in to some range-inspired flashlight position. Move your light to exploit your surroundings as much as you can. That may mean shining the light above your head or off to the side, or it may mean using a standard flashlight position at your centerline.

There are other artificial tools you may want to try in the FOF environment. One of these is a night vision device. These are becoming more and more accessible as new technology replaces old. As with anything else, the better units command higher prices. I would rather buy a $300 night vision device than a $200 flashlight.

FINAL WORDS

Stay sharp, stay alert, and always be ready . . . your Final Exam may come at any moment.

The information in this book is very important because, whether you are a cop, a soldier, or a barber, FOF training will make you a better fighter. And make no mistake; our nation needs fighters.

There is much going on in the news every day about homeland security and terrorist threats. America is worried, and it should be. There are evil people just over the horizon, probably in our nation already as I type this, who are bent on our wholesale destruction. They are not like us; they do not look at life like we do, nor do they have the same values as we do. They cannot be bargained with unless you consider your own death as part of the bargain. They can only be defeated through personal readiness and the capacity for justified violence. Many people point to our uniformed officials as the ones who will defeat the enemy. I say that only coincidentally will they be the ones.

Think of how often a police officer happens to be right there on the scene when something bad happens. Then look at how many private citizens are usually there. It wasn't a platoon of police that thwarted the tangos aboard United Flight 93 on 9/11, and it was not a squad of air marshals that tackled and restrained "Shoe Bomber" Richard Reid. It was a group of courageous civilians with the capacity for controlled violence.

When the first post-911 terrorist event is thwarted midstream in the United States, it will probably be done by an armed private citizen with a concealed-carry permit and skills developed through training such as I have discussed in this book. Will it be you?

In my opinion, homeland security has been on the books since 1776. It's called the Second Amendment, and its troops are the many private citizens who carry firearms with them every day of their lives.

There are those in the training community who do not trust civilians. It really bothers them that you can read a book such as this and study the things herein. They prefer to withhold all such knowledge from anyone who doesn't have a badge or wear a uniform. They forget about such things as the Constitution, freedom, and the fact that the odds of a policeman being right there at the very moment you are attacked by the evil ones are about like those of winning the Powerball 10 times in a row with the same numbers.

They also forget that we in America are a prickly bunch and do not want to be protected by forfeiture of freedom. Being "protected" in that way goes against everything we are. Rather we demand the ability and means to protect ourselves. We will accept nothing less. We do not want to live serving a police state. To the contrary, we want to live in freedom. And freedom only comes with the ability and willingness to fight to preserve it. So if this book and its availability bother anyone who has forgotten about the fundamental principles this nation was founded upon, I am delighted. More is to follow.

As for the rest of us, the test may be coming. Right now your enemy is training, hardening and sharpening his skills. He's getting ready to kill you. Don't let him do it when you meet. Train hard, stay sharp, and, God willing, we will get to train again soon.